TRIAL BY FIRE:

BURNING JEWISH BOOKS

SUSAN EINBINDER

TRIAL BY FIRE:

BURNING JEWISH BOOKS

Susan Einbinder

Lectures on Medieval Judaism
at Trinity University:
Occasional Papers, III

MEDIEVAL INSTITUTE PUBLICATIONS
WESTERN MICHIGAN UNIVERSITY
Kalamazoo, Michigan
2000

This publication was made possible by a grant from the endowment funds of the Jewish Federation of San Antonio and by a generous donation from Mrs. Perry Kallison.

Lectures on Medieval Judaism at Trinity University
III. (2000) Susan Einbinder

Second Printing 2003

Printed in the United States of America.

ISBN 1-58044-071-1

TRIAL BY FIRE:

BURNING JEWISH BOOKS

They who have been slain by the sword are better off
than those who dwell desolate without Torah....
(*Vikuah Rabbenu Yehiel*, 12)

On a Friday in June of 1242, a young Jewish student in Paris
watched the Talmud burn. Meir ben Baruch of Rothenburg had
come to Paris, probably from Mainz, to study with Rabbi Yehiel. In
Mainz he had studied with Rabbi Judah b. Solomon, a rabbinical
scholar who was related to Meir's family.[1] Rabbi Judah had also
studied with Rabbi Yehiel, so it is not surprising that his young
kinsman had come to the prestigious Parisian school, one of several
that had earned the northern French rabbis great fame.[2] These
schools had achieved especial renown before Meir was born, in the
days of Rabbi Jacob b. Meir ("Rabbenu Tam" – d. 1171). As the
leading Jewish authority in late twelfth-century France, Rabbenu
Tam and his school in Troyes had nurtured a generation of important scholars. These scholars – called Tosafists, after their hallmark
additions, or *tosafot*, to talmudic learning – then migrated to other
towns in northern France, England and Germany, where they estab-
lished their own schools and educated their own students.

Rather like a well-organized alumni group today, the graduates
of the Tosafist academies stayed in touch with each other and with

1

their teachers.[3] Their mutual interests were not merely academic. The Tosafists were the religious authorities whose rulings were responsible for much of the character of northern European Jewish life in this period. Some of them were also poets, and by writing for the synagogue, they could reach a far greater segment of the Jewish population than would ever sit and pore over Talmudic commentaries. As times grew harder, the Tosafist scholar-poets mobilized a specific type of poetry to communicate a specific set of ideals. In particular, martyrological poems that commemorated the victims of anti-Jewish violence were designed to present a model of resistance and fortitude in the face of persecution. But these poems were not just therapeutic responses to terror and loss; they were also polemical vehicles, embodying in the figures of the martyrs behaviors and beliefs that reinforced Jewish identity while expressing revulsion for Christian symbols and faith.

Because they were recited in the synagogue, these *piyyutim*, or liturgical poems, could have been heard by everyone present – and surely on the fast and holy days when they were recited (like the 9th of Av, the fast of Gedaliah, or Yom Kippur), the synagogue was full. Hearing and comprehension are, however, entirely different matters. Very few women knew Hebrew, and we may assume that the poets wrote chiefly for men. But even men would have had to struggle with this difficult and densely allusive poetry. Most Jewish males were literate, but the focus of Tosafist education was intensive talmudic study, the privileged activity of a small elite.[4] Accordingly, the martyrological laments demonstrate sensitivity to a range of listeners. The basic images in the poems – images of bravery, consolation, contempt and revenge – would have reverberated clearly to all. At the same time, the poems are a dazzling mosaic of biblical and rabbinic allusions. On this level, the listeners most likely to decode the verses were arguably the students themselves, who would have taken pleasure in cracking the puzzles of the texts as they absorbed their message. My concern here is with a poem written by one such student – Meir b. Baruch of Rothenburg, whose lament for the Talmud gives us some idea how he and his comrades heard the message their teachers tried to convey.

2

The Tosafists may have been especially concerned with bolstering the identity of their disciples, a concern we may understand better by considering the circumstances of these privileged young men. Overall, the physical and psychological pressures on the French communities took a particular toll on the elite scholars among them. By the mid-thirteenth century the days of glory for the Tosafists were gone, and the double impact of persecution and attrition confronted the rabbis. Indeed, the holy martyrs killed by mob violence or judicial execution included many scholars of greater or lesser prominence. Yom Tov Joigny, a poet and scholar, was a martyr of the York massacre in 1189. Elhanan, the son of Rabbi Isaac of Dampiere (the "Ri") was killed in 1184, midway through a commentary on a talmudic tractate.[5] Uri b. Joel HaLevi, one of a family of known scholars and poets, was burned in 1216 in Cologne. Towards the end of the century, martyrdom also awaited Mordecai b. Hillel, the loyal student of Meir of Rothenburg, who would visit him in prison and record his legal opinions.[6]

Death, however, was only one tragedy that could befall the scholar-rabbi. Conversion was also an option, and in the early thirteenth century, as the pressure on northern French Jews increased, so did the number of Jews who converted.[7] Jews who accepted conversion at sword-point, in terror for their lives, were one sort of problem, which has been amply discussed.[8] Not all Jews, however, converted at sword-point, and it was a terrible blow when a combination of Christian argument and Jewish misery convinced educated young men to abandon their faith.[9]

Young, educated Jews seem to have been at high risk.[10] Through business and intellectual contacts, they were constantly exposed to Christian society and its temptations, and the turbulent emotions and frustration we associate now with "adolescence" and young adulthood may have made humiliation harder to bear.[11] Furthermore, zealous converts who interpreted (and translated) Jewish texts to the Church were a serious problem. Nicholas Donin, whose letter to Pope Gregory IX in 1239 first accused the Talmud of blasphemy, was such a figure, and there were others as well.[12] I would like to suggest, therefore, that the poetry of martyrdom addressed Jewish young men in particular ways, and these ways were aimed at

3

reinforcing what today we would call "Jewish identity." It is no accident that the ideal martyr of Tosafist poetry was an idealized form of his readers: a man of learning, wealth, and good family, who would sacrifice them all for God. At the same time, the martyr defiantly reviled Christianity in graphic, even vulgar terms, which must have made an equally strong impression on adolescent minds.[13]

Conversion to Christianity would peak in the mid-century; a few decades earlier, perhaps, the magnitude of the crisis could not be foreseen.[14] Nor could the fact that it would peak. For us, therefore, young Meir in Paris provides an opportunity. He represents the group of students to whom the martyrological ideal and its anti-Christian polemic were arguably most directed. Even better, he gives us an idea of how he and his fellow students *heard* their teachers, because when he saw the Talmud burning, Meir wrote a poem. *Sha'ali serufah ba-esh* has been treated as an inspired literary invention, a unique instance of a martyrological lament whose martyrs are books. Certainly, the mythic quality of Meir's own life, his later fame as a scholar, and his tragic end predisposed scholars to see his Talmud lament as yet another tribute to an exceptional mind. Yet, however brilliant he was, the Meir of 1242 was still a young man with his fame and misfortune before him. Moreover, even a genius rarely invents something out of nothing. Let me, then, try to situate Meir's lament in a larger historical and literary context. Where did Meir get the idea to write a lament for burning books, and what can this poem's originality or conventionality tell us? Can we use Meir's poem to construct a fuller picture of Jewish life in the early thirteenth century?

In fact, Meir's poem is not unique; another long-forgotten lament commemorates the same event. Moreover, Meir's poem drew on a number of available literary traditions. These include Judah HaLevi's famous lament to Zion and its subsequent imitations, vernacular Christian poems to a female Beloved (particularly the Virgin), and earlier Jewish descriptions of the desecration of sacred texts. Finally, while the idea of burning books seems to have come from their Christian neighbors, angry factionalism within the Jewish world sometimes led Jews to burn books by other Jews.[15] These controversies – epitomized by the furor over books by Maimonides –

4

were sometimes documented in poetry, as we shall see. But let me start with Meir, and try to reconstruct the cultural and literary developments around him when he wrote.

Meir was born in Worms, probably around 1220-1223, as he was studying Talmud with Rabbi Isaac Or Zarua' in Würzburg in 1235.[16] From Würzburg, he went to Mainz to study with Rabbi Judah haCohen, who sent him on to Paris to study under Rabbi Yehiel (the head of the Paris academy), Rabbi Samuel ben Salomon of Falaise, Rabbi Ezra of Moncontour and Rabbi Samuel of Evreux.[17] Thus Meir b. Baruch was in all likelihood about 20 years of age when the burning of the Talmud took place.[18] Whether or not he was present for the "trial" of the Talmud and his teacher's role in its defense, he seems to have been an eye-witness to the outcome of the hearings.

The Church's interest in the Talmud was a recent development. When the apostate Nicholas Donin presented his charges against the Talmud to Gregory IX in 1239, "it seemed to have been news to the Pope" that the Jews relied on an extra-Scriptural book that contained blasphemies against Jesus and Mary as well as numerous other "errors" of belief.[19] This lack of earlier interest also characterized the monarchy, which until the late 1230s chiefly viewed its Jews as a source of potential income.[20]

Albeit novel, the official concern of both Louis IX and ecclesiastical leaders had grave consequences for French Jews. Donin provided Gregory IX with a list of 35 charges against the Talmud, according to which the Talmud contained numerous blasphemies against God, Jesus, Mary and Christianity. It was full of insulting and incredible fables, some of which portrayed God as manipulated by the rabbis. Moreover, it represented a perversion of the sense of the Bible until those who followed its dictates could no longer be considered "Jews," that is, the surviving remnant of biblical Israel which since Augustine of Hippo Christianity had held itself obligated to preserve as a witness in its midst.[21]

Gregory IX's letter to the monarchs of France, England, Aragon, Navarre, Castile, Leon and Portugal aroused enthusiasm only in royal France.[22] There Louis IX impounded Jewish books in a surprise Sabbath raid in the spring of 1240. A team of rabbis, headed by Rabbi Yehiel (Meir's teacher), was summoned hastily to defend the

Talmud in a series of sessions before an audience including King Louis IX, the Queen Mother (Blanche of Castile) and Queen Margaret. They were confronted by Nicholas Donin and a delegation of leading churchmen.[23] Technically neither a judicial trial nor an inquisitorial process, the "trial" that ensued was "*sui generis*, something new, but a possible precedent for the future."[24] Unsurprisingly, despite the efforts of Rabbi Yehiel and his colleagues, the Talmud was condemned in 1240 as a book containing heretical and blasphemous material, insulting to Christianity, and a deviation from biblical "Judaism." For two years, the rabbis managed to stave off the evil decree, but the forces arrayed against them were inexorable.[25] The Talmud was burned on Friday, the 6th of Tammuz by the Jewish calendar, in June of 1242.

Historians repeat (somewhat helplessly, as the report and its quantitative implications remain uncertain) the late thirteenth-century account of Rabbi Zedekiah bar Abraham, which describes "twenty-four wagons full of Talmuds, legal and aggadic texts" brought to be burned that June.[26] Over the next century, the official condemnation was reaffirmed, sometimes with burning, in 1247, 1248, 1254, 1284, 1290, 1299, 1319 and 1321.[27] It was not hard to foresee the consequences. The attack on the "Talmud" was indeed a blow to the heart of Tosafist education. Meir b. Baruch, like many Jewish students before him, had been taught that the Talmud was a sacred corpus of "Oral" Law, revealed to Moses along with the Written Law at Sinai. It was this combination of "Written" and "Oral" Law that most truly constituted the sacred Jewish teachings of "Torah." Far from constituting a deviation from their ancient Law, the Talmud was essential, as Rabbi Yehiel and his colleagues argued before the Crown, if Jews were to understand that Law at all.[28] Without it, Jewish life could not survive. The burning of the Talmud was a burning of the Law itself, a tragedy of unspeakable proportions even in the light of the human losses of those years.

By 1247, Meir would be back in Germany, settling in Rothenburg until his father's death in 1276 or 1281, when he returned to Worms.[29] In 1286, he was arrested in Lombardy, where he had stopped with his daughters and son-in-law en route to the Holy Land. Such emigration was illegal, as indeed was any migration of

Jews under the dominion of one lord to the territory of another.[30] Remanded to the custody of Rudolf I, the Hapsburg ruler, he was held in Ensisheim and Wasserburg until his death in 1293. Even then, it would be another seven years before Christian authorities turned over his body for Jewish burial.[31]

The poem *Sha'ali serufah ba-esh* ("Ask, O you who are burned in fire") undoubtedly owes some of its popularity to its model, HaLevi's famous lament for Zion, *Tsion halo tishali.* HaLevi's poem addresses a personified (feminine) Zion, for whom the speaker longs and whom he implores to attend to her yearning supplicants, whose devotion to her has not flagged through their years of suffering in exile. In a number of ways, Meir's poem evokes HaLevi's, formally by adhering to HaLevi's metrical and rhyme schemes, internally in linguistic echoes, and thematically in its poignant address to a feminized "Torah" whose devotees anguish over Her and their fates. The poems are identical in length and meter – a quantitative meter common in Sephardic poetry, but far rarer among the poets of northern France and Ashkenaz.[32] They also share a rhyme: –*ayikh,* the feminine pronominal suffix "your." We may recall HaLevi's opening line:

ציון הלא תשאלי על שלום אסיריך

Zion won't you ask about the fate of your captives?

Meir's poem begins:[33]

שאלי שרופה באש לשלום אבליך / המתאוים שכן בחצר זבוליך
השואפים על-עפר ארץ והכואבים / המשתוממים עלי מוקד גויליך
ההולכים חשכים ואין נגה, וקווים לאור / יומם, עליהם אשר ירח ועליך

O You who are burned in fire, ask how your mourners fare
They who yearn to dwell in the court of your dwelling place
They who gasp in the dust of the earth and who feel pain
They who are stunned by the blaze of your parchment.
They who walk in the dark with no light, but hope for the
     light
Of day to shine forth over them and you.

7

At least a half-dozen times, Meir draws deliberately on HaLevi's poem, alluding especially to verses in the second half describing Jewish suffering in exile. The evocations can be poignant, as when HaLevi's speaker longs to traverse the Holy Land, and to be "stunned" with awe at the tombs of his ancestors in Hebron and at the Mount beyond Jordan, while Meir's speaker is "stunned" by the blaze of parchment afire.[34] Both poets cry that it is impossible to eat or drink while their grief is so great – one because Israel is in the hands of her enemies, "dogs" who drag the "young lions" away (HaLevi, v. 39), and the other because "the plunderers" have "burned the Almighty's prize possession in the square" (Meir, v. 40). In both poems, the speakers plead for the faithful remnant "who clings to your cloak," respectively Zion's and Torah's (HaLevi, v. 55 and Meir, v. 46). Meir boldly raises the theological question with which learned Christian clerics and common folk alike repeatedly plied the Jews: Did not the New Law of the Christians supersede the Old Law of the Jews? He writes

> I will pour forth tears until like a river they reach
> Unto the tombs of your most noble princes,
> Moses and Aaron, on Mt. Hor, and I will ask: Is there
> A new Torah, that your scrolls may be burned? (vv. 29-32)

Were not Jewish abjection and degradation the surest sign that the old covenant of God and Israel had been abrogated? From the perspective of the Christian disputants at the Talmud trial, this was true in part because the Jews had corrupted biblical truth with their Oral Law. To Jews like the young Rabbi Meir, there was no difference between biblical (written) and talmudic (oral) law; both had been revealed at Sinai. As Meir laments, by "cutting down" the Tablets and then burning the Talmud, the Christians had responded with double folly to the twofold nature of the Law (vv. 35-36).

Perhaps the most striking feature of Meir's lament for the Talmud is that it is framed as an address to a female figure. Had Meir composed a lament merely to "Talmud," which is a masculine noun, he could not have employed this device. But by turning to a personification of "Torah," which is feminine, he emphasized the identity of "Torah" and "Talmud," while evoking longingly the feminine figure of his lament, a combination of Mothers Zion and Rachel. Where did he get this idea?

Long before Meir composed his lament, HaLevi's *Tsion halo tishali* had given birth to a genre of "Zion" poems, many still found in the liturgy for the Ninth of Av. Five examples written before 1240, following HaLevi's model, all address a feminine personification of "Zion."[35] Indeed, one original feature of Meir's lament is that it is addressed to a female figure who is *not* Zion. It seems likely that part of the appeal of these poems lay in their use of a feminine persona. And why not? A thriving vernacular tradition of courtly lyrics written by Christian poets for female figures must have shaped the aesthetic expectations and emotional sensibilities of Jewish listeners as well.[36] Some of these vernacular poems were dedicated to real (if idealized) women, and some to the female figure most sacred to Christian believers, the Virgin Mary.

A third kind of poetry, the crusade lyric (*sirventes*) could juxtapose both types of women, as in the poems of Thibaut of Champagne, a contemporary of Meir. The speaker in Thibaut's crusade songs is torn between his desire for his wife or lover and his desire to serve God, for whom he must travel to distant lands:

> Bien doi mes cuers estre liez et dolanz:
> dolanz de ce que je part de ma dame,
> et liez de ce que je sui desirranz
> de servir Dieu, qui est mes cuers et m'ame.
> Iceste amor est trop fine et puissanz....

> [It is fitting that my heart be joyous and doleful:
> Doleful for leaving my lady,
> And joyous, desirous
> Of serving God, who is my heart and my soul.
> This love is surpassingly true and powerful....]

In mingled devotion and despair, the crusader turns to the Virgin, who becomes a substitute for the woman he leaves behind:

9

Dame des ciez, granz roine puissanz,
au grant besoing me soiez secoranz!
De vos amer puisse avoir droite flamme,
quant dame pert, par dame me soit aidanz!

[Lady of the heavens, great, powerful queen,
Greatly am I in need of succor!
May I be inflamed with love for you!
When I lose a lady, by a lady may I be helped!][37]

By invoking "Lady Torah" in his lament, Meir shapes a Jewish counterpart to the female beloved of Christian song and offers a literary analogue to the Virgin herself. Here, indeed, we gain a sense of how the model of feudal, romantic love had made inroads into the Jews' spiritual world. In the hands of a young poet, it achieved an ardor and lyricism otherwise absent in medieval Hebrew verse from Christian Europe.[38] Meir's delicate allusions to Mother Rachel add even greater pathos to the more abstract female figure of "Torah." Alluding to Jeremiah's depiction of Rachel weeping for her children (Jer 31), Meir proclaims that his lady's suffering will not last forever:

Once again you will wear a crimson ornament, and take up
your timbrel
And go forth in dance, singing for joy in your dances (vv. 65-
66)

His listeners know he refers to the promise of Jeremiah 31:3:

I will yet rebuild you and you will be rebuilt, O Maid of Israel.
Once more you will take up your timbrel and go forth in
dance....

It is no wonder if scholars and readers have thought Meir's poem unique. In a sense, it is, just as any great poem is, but it remains the case that the idea of writing a lament for the burned Talmuds was not merely his own. A sixteenth-century *mahzor* (high

10

holiday prayer book) from Salonika preserves a penitential poem by an unknown poet named Solomon that also mourns the burning of the 6th of Tammuz.[39] The text is a bit tangled and the poetry not very good, but for our purposes it is important. Solomon's lament begins:[40]

> O sun and moon and stars of heaven, cry out and wail with-
> out rest[41]
> Like ostriches, forever, not for a day or two. Make mourning,
> eulogies and laments[42]
> For all knees turn to water,[43]
> My heart is broken and I am powerless[44]
> *For the Holy Torah on the 6th of Tammuz; let all the house*
> *of Israel weep for Tammuz.[45]*

Despite its obvious dissimilarities, Solomon's poem shares a few significant features with Meir's. Both poets wrote in metrical and stanzaic forms borrowed from Spanish Hebrew poetry. Solomon's lament also repeats a theme at the heart of Meir's poem. "Torah," for both men, is the combined repository of Written and Oral Law, and Solomon's refrain line affirms this by subsuming both under the rubric of "Torah." Moreover, like Meir, Solomon believes that the biblical covenant between God and Israel is mediated through rabbinic law. Without Torah, God's blueprint for the cosmos, the celestial order is unraveled. As Solomon says, the laws of heaven and earth "existed because of the covenant, and surely God's enemies have razed their foundations" (v. 7). Solomon calls on God to avenge them quickly, lest the Christians argue that He has abandoned the Jews and their Law.

The refrain line of Solomon's lament suggests that the poem was intended for a commemorative liturgy, likely the fast-day declared to mark the burning. It illustrates that it was not novel for a Jewish writer to have thought of adapting the conventions of lament poetry to describe the burning and desecration of books. To do so, Jewish writers also drew on conventions for describing book desecrations. So, let us turn to the ways Hebrew poets before them had

11

described the destruction of sacred texts. How do these influence our poems?

A survey of medieval Hebrew martyrological poems reveals some fifteen laments that describe the desecration of sacred texts.[46] The laments range from poetic accounts of First Crusade violence (1096) to the Rindfleisch massacres of 1298; one poem may be as late as 1327, although one might also argue it is a thirteenth-century composition.[47] Three laments are from 1096 and one commemorates the martyrs of Speyer killed in the wake of Third Crusade violence in 1196. But the majority of these poems (ten) document thirteenth-century incidents.

Certain motifs recur in these poems. All but one of the laments describe incidents of mob violence that combined attacks on Jews – men, women and children – and on sacred texts – Torah scrolls and sometimes other books also. The mobs are not specifically looking for rabbinic texts; on the contrary, they attack what they find in the synagogue, usually the scrolls in the ark. As there would be no reason for Christians to destroy Torah scrolls (containing the Pentateuch) for their content, it is their role as cultic objects that targets them for desecration.

The 1096 laments set a standard for later poets, describing the Torah in terms of endearment, always feminine, and the horror of seeing "her" torn open and defiled, trampled and dragged through the mud. Sometimes the Torah and study-house are described as a *miqdash*, the biblical Temple. Two poems describe scrolls converted to degrading use, in one case made into shoes for lepers and in another perhaps drum covers.[48] One 1096 lament alludes to the midrashic legend in which Jewish children were wrapped in their books and slaughtered.[49] Mordecai bar Eleazer's lament for the burning of Uri HaLevi in Cologne (1216) depicts Uri dismembered and then burned while wrapped in a scroll, a clear allusion to the Talmudic story of Hananiah (or Haninah) ben Teradion, one of the famed "Ten Martyrs" of the Hadrianic persecutions, who was burned wrapped in a Torah scroll.[50]

A 1096 lament by Kalonymous bar Judah echoes in many later poems, including Meir's and Solomon's. Kalonymous mourns "the beautiful young maidens and the tender young boys / wrapped in

12

their books and dragged to slaughter." These books are not just Torah scrolls. And since this is long before any official attack on rabbinic literature, Kalonymous does not mind distinguishing between biblical and rabbinic literature:

> I saw Her torn, bereft and solitary
> Torah and Scripture and Mishnah and Aggadah.
> Answer this, and lament and tell me:
> Where are Torah and Talmud and those who study her?[51]

Kalonymous cries out "brokenly and bitterly" for the unanticipated attack on Jewish learning:

> On the day the Law was given, I was prepared to rejoice:
> [But] on the day she was given, just so she returned;
> She went up to heaven to her dwelling-place
> With her covering and sheath and those who study and seek
> her
> Her students and teachers by light and dead of night.[52]

Kalonymous bar Judah's lament must have enjoyed a good degree of fame. It is the only poem of all the earlier laments to mention books that echoes directly in both Meir's and Solomon's laments for the Talmud. Meir also asked if the auto da fé signaled a reversal of Sinai, and whether the covenant was dead:

> ... Is there
> A new Torah, that your scrolls may be burned?
> Born on the third month, and the fourth was arranged for
> Destroying your grace and the beauty of your crown. (vv. 31-
> 34)

Solomon, too, echoed Kalonymous when he bewailed the Torah (the "Light of Life") that "has been taken away and gone up to heaven" (v. 16).

Thus Meir did have a precedent for some of the motifs he used in his lament for the Talmud. Kalonymous' poem in particular seems to have resonated deeply. Still, none of these earlier descriptions of burned books appears in a lament dedicated solely to books, and only one commemorates a scroll and martyr executed judicially and not at the hands of a mob. In this respect, the source for Meir's inspiration did not apparently lie in earlier martyrological conventions. But there is another source of poetry specifically about books that he would likely have known. Moreover, that poetry also described books on trial and books that were burned. I refer to the Maimunist controversy of the 1230s, which although usually discussed with respect to the abundant and vituperative correspondence left by the disputants, generated poetic commentary as well. To this we now turn.

As scholars have reconstructed it, the Maimunist controversy did not originally have anything to do with the rabbis of northern France. How exactly they became embroiled in a dispute between rabbinic factions in Provence and Spain, and what part they played in the uproar that ensued have been considerably debated.[53] What seems clear is that in 1230, a rabbi in Montpellier, Solomon b. Abraham, tried to enlist the support of northern French rabbis in his battle to ban the works of Maimonides. The specific works that were contested were the great philosopher's *Guide to the Perplexed* and his *Book of Knowledge* (or Science); the former had recently been translated from Arabic into Hebrew by Samuel ibn Tibbon and was circulating in southern France.[54] Solomon accused Maimonides' works of leading Jews to apostasy by emphasizing allegorical interpretation and rational philosophy.

Which French rabbis Solomon approached (perhaps through his students, Jonah Gerondi and David bar Saul), and how much familiarity they actually had with Maimonides' writings are not clear. *Some* of these rabbis responded by issuing a ban (*herem*) on the works of Maimonides and all "Greek" (philosophical) science. Amazingly, the ban applied to all Jews in all lands for all time. In retaliation, a group of pro-Maimunist rabbis in Provence sent an ambassador to Catalonia to urge a counter-ban; that ambassador was David Qimhi ("Radaq"), the famed exegete from Narbonne. As the controversy escalated, a number of French rabbis reversed themselves on their ban, while others may have excommunicated Qimhi.

14

According to Solomon bar Abraham, he was threatened by the Jews in Orléans and Béziers, and he turned in desperation to the Christian authorities, asking them to review the offending books. His opponents accused him bitterly of betraying the works of their master.

Maimonides' books were burned in 1232. Despite Hillel of Verona's claim that the burning occurred in Paris, most scholars believe that only one conflagration took place, in Montpellier. Hillel was writing nearly sixty years after the event, and not necessarily for historical accuracy.[55] Intriguingly, he associates the burning of 1232 with that of the Talmud ten years later (events he believes to be separated in time by a mere forty *days*). For Hillel, the burning of the Talmud in Paris was God's way of punishing the French rabbis for their role in the attack on Maimonides' writings. For those who doubted that God would account 1,200 volumes of Talmud and midrashic learning the equivalent price of the *Guide* and *Book of Knowledge*, Hillel averred that "Rabbenu Moses" (ben Maimon) "was practically a second Moses to his generation, and all the righteousness of the generation depended upon him:[56]

> And do not be surprised if the Holy One, Blessed be He, punished the Law [Torah] of the French Jews on behalf of Rabbenu Moses, or that He did not have mercy on their books of Talmud. Rather, He appeared over them in a pillar of fire and cloud until He roused all the clerics against them and the great persecutions were renewed. Communities were slaughtered, more than 3000 [Jews], and their Talmuds were given to burning and blaze. Then the decree went forth that they should no longer openly study Talmud until the present day. And if you ask how we know that the persecutions were related to the burning of the *Guide* and the *Book of Knowledge*, I will answer you that the sign and proof are that not forty days elapsed between the burning of our teacher's books and the burning of the Talmud. Moreover, they were burned in the very same place, all the compilations and commentaries to be found in Paris, so that the ashes of the Talmud mingled with the ashes of the *Guide* and the *Book of Knowledge*, for those ashes were still there....[57]

15

The voluminous correspondence that flew between representatives of the Jewish communities in Spain, Provence and northern France has survived in a lopsided fashion: almost all of the surviving letters represent Maimonides' defenders, and they often provide polemical more than factual accounts. It is not my intent here to render judgment on the thorny issues posed by the letters and their utility in reconstructing events. For our purposes, however, several points should be made. First, the above passages suggest the striking degree to which martyrological imagery and language have penetrated to very different sorts of writing by the late thirteenth century. In other words, not merely can a case be made for the influence of the Maimunist controversy on Meir of Rothenburg in 1242, but also for the reciprocal observation that the martyrocentrism of Ashkenaz and northern French Jewry had an impact on Jewish writers in Spain and Provence.[58] In fact, this influence can be documented while the controversy still raged, for instance in a letter from the Ibn Hisdai brothers, two of Maimonides' defenders, where we read:

> They [the anti-Maimunists] turned over the *Book of Knowledge* and the *Guide* to the priests, the Major and Minorite friars. They said to them: "Why do you wear yourselves out going to the ends of the earth and wandering the distant sea, chasing after heretics to your law in order to burn the evil in your midst? Behold, here we, too, have books, books of heretics and apostates, called *Knowledge* and the *Guide*, which have blood on their hands. You are obligated to guard us from stumbling as much as yourselves, so arise and go out against them....[59]

Jewish descriptions of crusader attacks in 1096 had made a remarkably similar rhetorical point. Compare this excerpt from the chronicle of Solomon bar Samson:

> As [the crusaders] passed through the villages where there were Jews, they said to each other: "Here we travel a distant path seeking ... to avenge ourselves on the Ishmaelites. But behold, here are the Jews who dwell in our midst and whose ancestors

16

killed and crucified [Jesus] for no reason. Let us avenge ourselves
upon them first....[60]

The Ibn Hisdai brothers also report that popular scorn for
Solomon and his friends found expression in a satirical ditty, which
they quote. The jingle alludes to the rumor, perhaps spread by the
Maimunists, that Solomon b. Abraham and his friends were subse-
quently arraigned by the Christian courts for providing false testi-
mony and sentenced to have their tongues cut out:

> Those who opposed and betrayed the *Guide* were teachers of
>   no worth
> Because they were deceitful, God hit them where it hurt:
> Their mouths were turned to Heaven – but their tongues went
>   down to earth.[61]

It is unlikely that "popular scorn" produced a skilful poem in
the satirical tradition of aristocratic Spanish poetry. Nonetheless,
here is evidence that the battle over Maimonides' books was fought
in verse as well as in prose. Moreover, Meir of Rothenburg could
have read some of this literature, as a selection of the letters were
collected and published in 1234 in Abraham b. Azriel's *Arugat
haBosem*.[62] But letters and jingles were not the only literature the
controversy generated. One of Maimonides' detractors wrote serious poems, and some were addressed to his books.

The poet Meshullam DaPiera was a friend of Rabbi Moses b.
Nahman (Nachmanides, or the "Ramban") from Gerona. In some
senses a peacemaker between the contending parties, Nachmanides
was offended by the hubris of the northern French rabbis who pre-
sumed to declare a ban effective beyond their boundaries, but he
was sympathetic to the anti-Maimunist declarations ascribed to
them. Unlike his friend the Ramban, however, DaPiera wasted few
words on diplomacy, and his poetry found a wide audience.
DaPiera wrote several poems attacking the works of Maimonides
and praising Solomon b. Abraham of Montpellier and the northern
French rabbis who had gone to war against them.[63] Two poems spe-

17

cifically address a personified *Guide to the Perplexed*. In one scathing couplet, DaPiera writes:

מורה נבוכים החרש פיך בלום, הן הדברים לא שמענום עד הלום
ישאו עונם אומרים כי הכתב משל והנביא אשר אתו חלום

> O *Guide to the Perplexed,* be silent and shut your mouth!
> These are things we have never heard before now.
> Those who say that Scripture is allegory, and its Prophet
> [a man of] dreams, shall bear their sin.[64]

And in a longer poem:

מורה נבוכים לנבואות עמך / מדון ומלחמה בך יתגרו

> O *Guide to the Perplexed,* Prophecy has a quarrel with you
> and will challenge you to war.
> Your book has said original things, their likes unwritten and
> unmentioned in legends,
> It banishes signs and omens and describes their Creator's
> wonders as fashioned.
> O how they have undone the bonds of my faith, and without
> hands have untied the laces of my books!
> They have taken and belittled a precious stone from the
> necklace, and the necklace stones have been scat-
> tered.[65]

Unsurprisingly, the fanatical self-righteousness that character-ized the so-called Maimunist controversy spilled over to the ranks of lesser-known scholars as well. In the early thirteenth century, osten-sibly motivated by a (strong) distaste for anthropomorphisms, a rabbi named Abba Shalom recorded with satisfaction his successful incineration of an offending text.[66] Around the same time, one of the works of the great Spanish Hebrew writer, Judah ibn Shabbetai, was burned in Saragossa and lost forever.[67] The phenomenon may have been more common than is generally thought.

18

In sum, a number of rich literary traditions stood at Meir's disposal when he composed his lament for the Talmud in 1242. Some of those came from a martyrological repertoire and some came from very different sorts of writing, but together they imply a universe of poetic possibility from which a gifted young poet could draw, adapt and innovate to create something "new." The result was an elegiac and yet polemical blend of longing and sorrow that reflected the centrality of rabbinic learning in the world of the academy. At the same time, when viewed in its proper context, Meir's lament also refracts through its sources some of the factionalized and fractious world in which it was written, a time when the glory of kings and churchmen was less than glorious for their Jews. Uncertainty and a sense of siege may be especially difficult emotions for a young man to suffer, and we sense them stirring in the anguished frustration that echoes through Meir's polemic of desire.

Jewish learning, as we have seen, was under concerted attack. Over the thirteenth century, the scattered poetic remains that document persecutions against Jews in royal France often refer to burning books. Other texts are cited as proof of the resulting Jewish book shortage.[68] How much this shortage was limited to France may ironically be gleaned from a later complaint of Meir of Rothenburg himself. In prison from 1286 until his death in 1293, the venerable scholar continued to write and work. Significantly, his complaints about library resources concern his conditions in imprisonment only; he gives no indication that his personal difficulties in obtaining books were shared by the Jewish scholars of Ashkenaz.[69]

The Talmud was condemned repeatedly over the coming years, and the conflagrations – fed by decreasing numbers of books – would recur. In 1320, Pope John XXII issued yet another bull calling for the confiscation and burning of the Talmud. The Jews of France petitioned him to relent but to no avail; in 1321, the bishop of Pamiers, Jacques Fournier, had the Talmud burned there, and again during Lent in Paris.[70] In this case, a fast-day liturgy the Jews recited to save their books still survives, in an Italian *mahzor* dated to 1420.[71] Unremarkable in most respects, the liturgy is nonetheless touching in its repeated and anxious invocations to *El hanish-kakhot*, the Lord of the forgotten. Indeed, the play of forgetfulness

19

and memory throughout the liturgical passages is striking. If the expression reflects the petitioners' fear that God has forgotten them, its insistent repetition suggests the fear that without their books, the Jews will no longer remember themselves. Indeed, what is threatened with the loss of their books is the fragile weave of sacred and social history wrought by learning and memory.

Meir the young poet may have captured the tone of mourning and bereavement following the events of 1242 in ways an older, more mature poet – even an older, more mature Meir – could not have. The polemical and satirical restlessness of DaPiera's poems, the exquisite lyrical imagery of HaLevi's Zionide lament, the longing devotion to the Beloved of vernacular songs, all fuse in a remarkable tribute to Jewish study and students. In 1242, the Jews of France stood, not at Sinai, but at the brink of its possible reversal. When the tide finally turned, or what gave the tired and battered communities new strength to resist the forces against them, is not clear. But by the 1270s, it would be clear to the Crown and the Church that their strategy to convert the Jews had not succeeded. Surely, one of the reasons was the power of their teachers; another was the faith of their students. And let us not forget the books they treasured, and the poems that tell us why.

National Humanities Center; March, 2000

APPENDIX

Meir ben Baruch of Rothenburg
"Sha'ali serufah ba-esh"[72]

O You who are burned in fire, ask how your mourners fare,[73]
They who yearn to dwell in the temple of your dwelling
    place,
They who gasp in the dust of the earth and who feel pain,[74]
They who are stunned by the blaze of your parchment,[75]
5   They who walk in the dark with no light, but hope for the
    light[76]
Of day to shine forth over them and you.
How fare the people sighing and weeping and broken-
    hearted,
Continually lamenting your birth pains?[77]
They mourn like jackals and ostriches
10   And call for bitter wailing on your behalf.
How could she who was given by the flaming God be con-
    sumed by the fire[78]
Of mortals, while the foes were not scorched by your em-
    bers?[79]
(And you, how long will you dwell in tranquility, O dainty
    foe?[80]
Have not your thorns covered my flowers?[81]
15   You sit proudly to judge God's children with all
Judgments and bring them to trial.
Moreover, you decree burning for the law and regulations
    given in fire –
Happy the one who requites you![82])
Did my Rock [appear] in flame and fire to give you[83]
20   Later to another fire to blaze at your hems?
O Sinai, was this why the Lord chose you, disdaining

21

Greater mountains to shine within your borders?
To be a sign of the Law when her glory would dwindle
And go down? Let me make an analogy:
25 You are like a king who wept at his son's feast-day
Foreseeing his death – so your speech foretold your end.[84]
O Sinai, instead of your cloak, let your garment be a sack.
Don the garb of widows instead of your dresses.
I will pour forth tears until like a river they reach
30 Unto the tombs of your most noble princes,
Moses and Aaron, on Mt. Hor, and I will ask: Is there[85]
A new Torah, that your scrolls may be burned?
Born on the third month, and the fourth was arranged for
Destroying your grace and the beauty of your crown.[86]
35 For [the foe] has cut down the Tablets, then doubled his folly[87]
By burning the Law in fire – are these your twofold dam-
       ages?[88]
I wonder to myself: How can food taste sweet
After seeing how they gathered your booty[89]
As though it were idolatrous property, and those whom you
       had rejected
40 From your community burned the Almighty's prize posses-
       sion in the square?[90]
I do not know how to find the way to you.
Your ways, the path of righteousness, are mourning.[91]
A drink mixed with tears would taste sweeter than honey
And to be bound in your chains would be sweet to my feet!
45 It would soothe my eyes to draw forth tears until
There were no more for those who cling to the hem of your
       cloak.[92]
But they burn dry as they go down my cheeks, for
I am so moved by the wandering of your Master.
He took his wealth and went far away[93]
50 And with him your protection fled.[94]
And I remained behind alone, like one bereft and solitary,[95]
Like the mast at the top of your tower.[96]
No more will I hear the voice of men and women singing,[97]
For the cords of your pipes have been severed.[98]

55 I will dress and cover myself in sackcloth, for very dear to me
Were the souls of your slain ones, who have multiplied and
grown like the sand.[99]
I wonder greatly at the light of day, which shines [100]
On all, but brings darkness to you and me.
Cry aloud bitterly for your destruction and for your [101]
60 Anguish – if only He would recall the love of your wedding
day![102]
Gird on sackcloth for the conflagration that
Was kindled to divide you and decimate your hilltops![103]
The Rock will console you in compensation for your suffering,
He will restore from captivity[104]
The tribes of Jeshurun, and raise you up from degradation.[105]
65 Once again you will wear a crimson ornament, and take up
your timbrel[106]
And go forth in dance, singing for joy in your dances.
My heart will be lifted up when I see the Rock shed light upon
you
Bringing light into your darkness and illuminating your shad-
ows.[107]

Notes

1 There have been several biographical studies of Meir of Rothenburg that differ considerably in their interpretation of the later part of his life, but maintain consistency (perhaps due to a relative lack of interest) in the treatment of his youth. See Ephraim Urbach, *Ba'alei haTosafot* (Jerusalem: Mosad Bialik, 1955), esp. 401-46; J. Wellecsz, "Meir b. Baruch de Rothenbourg," *Revue des études juives* 59 (1903), 226-40; and Irving Agus, *Rabbi Meir of Rothenburg: His Life and His Works as Sources for the Religious, Legal, and Social History of the Jews of Germany in the Thirteenth Century*, 2 vols. (Philadelphia: Dropsie College, 1947). Agus' reconstruction of Meir's life, and particularly his development as a legal scholar, are based on a hypothetical dating of undated responsa and hence treated skeptically by modern scholars. Nonetheless, his treatment of Meir's youth in the small first chapter (1:3-13) is similar to Urbach's and Wellecsz'.

2 For Judah as a student of R. Yehiel's, see Wellecsz, "Meir b. Baruch," 235.

3 See Simha Goldin, " 'Companies of Disciples' and 'Companies of Colleagues': Communication in Jewish Intellectual Circles," in *Communication in the Jewish Diaspora*, ed. Sophia Menache (Leiden: Brill, 1996), 127-40.

4 Contrast the situation in nearby Germany, where educational efforts targeted the "primary" levels of schooling; see Ephraim Kanarfogel, *Jewish Education and Society in the High Middle Ages* (Detroit: Wayne State Univ. Press, 1993).

5 Haym Soloveitchik, "Catastrophe and Halakhic Creativity: Ashkenaz – 1096, 1242, 1306 and 1298," *Jewish History* 12.1 (1998), 74; Urbach, *Ba'alei haTosafot*, 211.

6 Mordecai, the author of the important compilation known by his name (the *Sefer haMordecai*), was killed in 1289. See Urbach, *Ba'alei haTosafot*, 436.

7 For a general history of the period, see Robert Chazan, *Medieval Jewry in Northern France: A Political and Social History* (Baltimore and London: Johns Hopkins Univ. Press, 1973) and William C. Jordan, *The French Monarchy and the Jews: From Philip Augustus to the Last Capetians* (Philadelphia: Univ. of Pennsylvania Press, 1989).

8 The convert who reverted to Judaism now fell under the aegis of the Church and was treated as a heretic; any Jew who was suspected of abetting him or her in returning to Judaism was liable to prosecution, as well. See Yosef Yerushalmi, "The Inquisition and the Jews in the Time of Bernard Gui," *Harvard Theological Review* 63.3 (1970), 317-76.

9 Shortly after 1240, in a religious debate staged in Narbonne, the Archbishop asked his Jewish disputant, Meir b. Simon, to explain how he could resist the obvious veracity of Christianity when so many learned and prominent Jews were abandoning Jewish error for the truth. He, too, should join the "intelligentsia" and convert with them. Meir's disputation is preserved in Parma, Biblioteca Palatina, MS. Parma 2749 (De Rossi 155), along with the famous letter he wrote to King Louis protesting the ban on Jewish usury (following the Melun ordinance of 1230). The manuscript, over

24

200 folios, has never been fully published. See Siegfried Stein, *Jewish-Christian Disputations in Thirteenth-Century Narbonne, An Inaugural Lecture Delivered at University College London 22 October 1964* (London: H.K. Lewis & Co., 1969), 1-27, esp. p. 21; and *idem*, "A Disputation on Moneylending between Jews and Gentiles in Me'ir b. Simeon's Milhemeth Miswah," *Journal of Jewish Studies* 10 (1959): 45-61; and for a partial Hebrew text, with introduction, Moses Judah HaCohen Blau, ed., *Sefer haMe'orot veSefer haHashlamah* (New York: n. p., 1964), 11-21. For the impact of the *stabilimentum* of 1223 and the ordinance of 1230, see Jordan, *French Monarchy*, 129-33.

[10] Ivan Marcus, "Martyrdom in Ashkenaz and the Story of R. Amnon of Mainz" [in Hebrew], in *Qedushat haHayim veHeruf haNefesh*, ed. Isaiah Gafni and Aviezer Ravitzky (Jerusalem: Merkaz Zalman Shazar le-toldot Yisrael, 1993), 131-47. Common sense also suggests the strategical value of prominent converts. Christian missionizing policy in the New World would later draw upon its experience at home, and New World missionaries also tried to win over figures of local prominence to Christianity; see Kenneth Mills, *Idolatry and Its Enemies: Colonial Andean Religion and Extirpation* (Princeton: Princeton Univ. Press, 1997).

[11] See William C. Jordan, "Adolescent Conversion in the Middle Ages: A Research Agenda," in *In the Shadow of the Millennium*, Notre Dame Conferences in Medieval Studies, ed. Michael A. Signer and John van Engen (Notre Dame, IN: Notre Dame Univ. Press, forthcoming); and the other sources cited in note 14 below; see also my "Faith and Fury: Jewish Martyrological Literature and Resistance to Conversion," paper presented at the Shelby Collum Davis Center at Princeton University, Dec. 3, 1999.

[12] He was, in fact, excommunicated by R. Yehiel around 1225; see *Vikuah Rabbenu Yehiel miParis*, ed. Reuven Margaliot ([Brooklyn, NY]: Ateret Publ., 1974-1975), 15. Other cases are well known: besides Donin, who was assisted by at least one other convert, Pablo Christiani was called from Spain by Louis IX to preach to his Jews in 1269; the stories of Herman the Jew, Abner of Burgos, and other prominent (and polemical) converts and their roles in the new missionizing have received much study. See Robert Chazan, *Daggers of Faith: Thirteenth-Century Christian Missionizing and Jewish Response* (Berkeley: Univ. of California Press, 1989); Jeremy Cohen, *The Friars and the Jews: The Evolution of Medieval Anti-Judaism* (Ithaca, NY: Cornell Univ. Press, 1982); *idem*, *Living Letters of the Law: Ideas of the Jew in Medieval Christianity* (Berkeley: Univ. of California Press, 1999), 334-42 (the section on "Friar Paul Christian and the Second Disputation in Paris,"); see also Jacob Mann, "La Lettre Polémique de Jacob b. Elie à Pablo Christiani," *Revue des études juives* 82 (1926), 363-77.

[13] Einbinder, "Faith and Fury."

[14] Jordan, *French Monarchy*, 150-52, relying on royal subsidies to converts, notes the increase in the 1250s and 1260s; see also J. Shatzmiller, "Converts to Christianity in Medieval Europe: 1200-1500," in *Cross-Cultural Convergences in the Crusader Period*, ed. Michael Goodich, Sophia Menache, and Sylvia Schein (New

25

York: P. Lang, 1995), 297-318. The number of papal letters that deal with the problem of subsidies for converts, or converts who relapse, also increases during this period; see Solomon Grayzel, *The Church and the Jews in the XIIIth Century*, vol. 2, *1254-1314*, ed. Kenneth R. Stow (New York: Jewish Theological Seminary in America; Detroit: Wayne State Univ. Press, 1989); and see the formularies published by Grayzel, in "Jewish References in a Thirteenth-Century Formulary," *Jewish Quarterly Review* 46 (1955), 44-65. David Berger has noted the changed tone in Jewish polemical literature (from self-confidence to anxiety). He claims that the *Sefer Yosef haMeqanne* of Joseph Official, R. Yehiel's student and the author of the Hebrew account of the Talmud trial, was directed primarily to apostates; see David Berger, "Mission to the Jews and Jewish-Christian Contacts in the Polemical Literature of the High Middle Ages," *American Historical Review* (1986), 591. See also Yerushalmi, "The Inquisition and the Jews," 326, 334-35.

[15] Shohet describes an ecclesiastical hearing in Paris that condemned to the flames a heretical (Christian) work, followed in 1225 by the burning of the books of John the Scot, the confiscation of books by one David de Dinant, and the prohibition of Aristotle's *Metaphysics* at the University of Paris. See Azriel Shohet, "Clarifications Concerning the First Maimunist Controversy" [in Hebrew], *Tarbiz* 36 (1971), 35.

[16] Wellecsz, "Meir b. Baruch," 227, 232; Agus, *Rabbi Meir of Rothenburg*, 1:7.

[17] Wellecsz, "Meir b. Baruch," 237; Agus, *Rabbi Meir of Rothenburg*, 1:9; Urbach, *Ba'alei haTosafot*, 410.

[18] Kanarfogel, *Jewish Education and Society*, 18 (and see n. 14 on 121-22), weighs the evidence pro and con, but also concludes that "Rabbi Meir of Rothenburg ... was perhaps ten when he studied with R. Isaac Or Zarua' for the first time," which would make him even younger than my estimate when he arrived in Paris.

[19] Solomon Grayzel, *The Church and the Jews in the XIIIth Century: A Study of their Relations During the Years 1198-1254, Based on the Papal Letters and the Conciliar Decrees of the Period* (Philadelphia: Dropsie College, 1933), 29.

[20] William C. Jordan, *The French Monarchy*, 136-37.

[21] The story has been discussed abundantly. See I. Baer, "Towards a Critique of the Disputations of R. Yehiel of Paris and R. Moses ben Nahman," [in Hebrew] *Tarbiz* 2 (1931), 172-87; J.M. Rosenthal, "The Talmud on Trial: The Disputation at Paris in the year 1240," *Jewish Quarterly Review* 47 (1956), 58-76, 145-69; Ch. Merchavia, *HaTalmud bere'i hanatsrut* (Jerusalem: Mosad Bialik, 1970), 227-360; Joel E. Rembaum, "The Talmud and the Popes: Reflections on the Talmud Trials of the 1240s," *Viator* 13 (1982), 203-23; Gilbert Dahan, "La Disputation de Paris 1240," *Communauté Nouvelle* 49 (1990), 98-120; William C. Jordan, "Marian Devotion and the Talmud Trial of 1240," in *Religionsgespräche im Mittelalter*, ed. Bernard Lewis and Friedrich Niewöhner (Wiesbaden: Harrassowitz, 1992), 61-76; and most recently Jeremy Cohen, *Living Letters*, 317-64. Solomon Grayzel has provided both the rele-

vant papal bulls and introductory essays in *The Church and Jews in the XIIIth Century* (see above, nn. 14, 19).

[22] Rosenthal, "The Talmud on Trial," 70.

[23] The delegation included Eudes of Chateauroux, Chancellor of the University of Paris; Walter, the Archbishop of Sens; William of Auvergne, the Bishop of Paris; Geoffrey of Bellevelle, Chaplain to the King; and Adam of Chambly, the Bishop of Senlis. Rosenthal, "The Talmud on Trial," 71; *Vikuah Rabbenu Yehiel*, 6.

[24] Jordan, "Marian Devotion," 65-66. As Jordan notes there, the "trial" does not "conform to 'inquisitorial' practice, which in any case was hardly fixed, given the fact that the Inquisition was only a few years old and its procedures inchoate. Nor was there any reason that the French government would opt to employ an ecclesiastical process ... in a forum under the presidency of the crown."

[25] *Vikuah Rabbenu Yehiel.* Merchavia, *HaTalmud,* contains a Hebrew translation of the Latin record, as well. The Latin was included in Isidore Loeb's early article, "La controvèrse de 1240 sur le Talmud," *Revue des études juives* 2 (1881), 252-70 and 3 (1881), 39-55. The Latin source is Paris, Bibliothèque Nationale, MS Latin 16558; for a brief description and excerpts translated into French, see Gilbert Dahan, "La disputation de Paris 1240," *Communauté nouvelle* 49 (1990), 107.

[26] Urbach, *Ba'alei haTosafot,* 375, citing the *Shibbolei haLeqet,* siman 263.

[27] Jordan, *French Monarchy,* 72, lists all these dates except the last, for which, see below, p. 19.

[28] *Vikuah Rabbenu Yehiel,* 13.

[29] Urbach, *Ba'alei haTosafot,* 410. Agus assumed that R. Meir remained in Rothenburg until his departure in 1286 and subsequent arrest; see *Rabbi Meir of Rothenburg,* vol. 1, n. 46 to p. 12. Wellecsz mentions the curious fact that Meir refused to visit his father (in Worms), which he attempts to interpret as a sign of respect (presumably, in other words, not to humiliate the father by outshining him); see "Meir b. Baruch," 230. Urbach, *Ba'alei haTosafot,* 406, discusses the various interpretations that have been offered for Meir's behavior, concluding also that the son sought to avoid embarrassing his father: "he knew that his father would judge himself harshly and would stand [i.e., in deference, and not sit] before his son, and in order to avoid this, he did not wish to encounter him." The explanation stretches credibility too far, I think. It seems to me more likely (and more interesting) that the brilliant and headstrong young son had a tense relationship with his less brilliant father, and turned his back on him upon his return from France.

[30] The legislation that permitted the extradition of Jews to the domain of the lord whose property they were legally considered to be (*tamquam proprium servum*) was approved in royal France in 1230 and by Rudolf sometime after his ascension to the throne in 1273; see Agus, *Rabbi Meir of Rothenburg,* 1:139, 143-44, where he argues the relevant legislation was passed in 1284. For royal France, see Jordan, *French Monarchy,* 136, and Gavin Langmuir, "Tanquam Servi: The Change in Jewish Status in French Law About 1200," in *Toward a Definition of AntiSemitism* (Berkeley: Univ. of California Press, 1990), 167-94.

[31] Urbach, *Ba'alei haTosafot*, 426; and see Agus, *Rabbi Meir of Rothenburg*, 1:125-57 (whose reconstruction is less reliable). As for the legend that holds that Meir's arrest was due to the prior arrest of a son, for whom he pledged a considerable ransom only to have the son bolt from prison, cited in the collected responsa of Haim Or Zarua' (no. 164), Urbach, *Ba'alei haTosafot*, 426, n. 14, comments that "there is no hint in all the literature of a son to R. Meir." In this context, it is worth noting that the son of Meir's teacher, R. Yehiel, was reportedly arrested around the time of the Talmud trial and vowed upon his release to emigrate to the Holy Land. His father released him from his vow until they could go together, which they did in approximately 1260. See Urbach, *Ba'alei haTosafot*, 378. Is it possible that the story of Yehiel and his son influenced later legends about the Maharam?

[32] See Abraham Grossman, "Contacts between Jewish communities in Spain and France" [in Hebrew] in *Galut Ahar Golah: Mehqarim betoldot 'am Ysrael Mugashim leProfessor Hayim Beinart*, ed. Aharon Mirski, Abraham Grossman, Yosef Kaplan (Jerusalem: Makhon Ben Tsvi leheqer qehillot Yisrael bamizrah, 1988), 75-101.

[33] The poem has been published in many places. I rely on the critical edition of Daniel Goldschmidt, in *Seder haQinot letish'ah be'Av* (Jerusalem: Mosad haRav Kook, 1972), 135-37. See also A. Habermann, *Gezerot ashkenaz vetsarefat* (Jerusalem: Mosad haRav Kook, 1945), 183-85; and Simon Bernfeld, *Sefer haDema'ot*, 3 vols. (Berlin: Eshkol, 1923-1926), 1:307-10. The lament also appears in the regular liturgy for the 9th of Av, see *Authorised Kinot for the Ninth of Av*, ed. Abraham Rosenfeld (London: n. p., 1965; reprint Jerusalem: C. Labworth & Co., 1970), 161-62, with a less than inspiring translation. The poem was translated by Robert Chazan in *Church, State and Jew in the Middle Ages* (New York: Behrman House, 1980), 229-31, although his translation contains several significant inaccuracies, and again by David Roskies in his *The Literature of Destruction: Jewish Responses to Catastrophe* (Philadelphia: Jewish Publication Society, 1988), 85-87. For my translation of the entire poem, see the Appendix. All translations in the present publication, unless otherwise indicated, are my own.

[34] The allusion hangs on the use of the verb *hishtomem*; see Judah HaLevi, *Tsion halo tishali* ("Zion won't you ask how your captives fare"), vv. 25-26, in *Ha-Shirah ha-'Ivrit bi-Sefarad uve-Provans*, ed. Hayim Shirman, 2nd ed. (Jerusalem: Mosad Bialik, 1960), 2:485-89, here 486-87; and Meir, ed. Goldschmidt, v. 3. On Meir's echo of HaLevi's phrase *hako'avim 'al shomemutekh* ("who feel pain over the desolation," vv. 49-50, p. 488), see below, n. 75.

[35] *Tsion, qehi kol tsari*, by Abraham Hozeh (12th cent.), in Rosenfeld, *Authorised Kinot for the Ninth of Av*, 154; *Tsion 'ateret tsvi*, by Eleazer haDarshan (d.1221), in Rosenfeld, 155-56; *Tsion yedidut yedid*, by Jacob (late 11th or early 12th cent.), in Rosenfeld, 158-60; *Tsion tsefirat pe'er*, by Meir ben Eleazer (early 13th cent.), in Rosenfeld, 163-65; *Tsion bemishpat lekhi*, by Joseph b. Jacob (11th cent.), in Rosenfeld, 165.

³⁶ It is unnecessary to "prove" that thirteenth-century French Jews would have known contemporary vernacular poetry. Their own vernacular was French, as their glosses and even liturgical compositions evidence; see D. Blondheim, "Contribution à l'étude de la poésie judéo-française," *Revue des études juives* 83 (1927), 22-51, 146-62; reprint as *Poèmes judéo-français au moyen âge* (Paris: H. Champion, 1927); and M. Banitt, "L'étude des glossaires bibliques des Juifs de France au Moyen Âge," *Proceedings of the Israel Academy of Science and Humanities* 2 (1967), 188-210; *idem*, "Les *poterim*," *Revue des études juives* 125 (1966), 21-33; and S. Einbinder, "The Troyes Laments: Jewish Martyrology in Hebrew and Old French," *Viator* 30 (1999), 201-30. Although it is southern, the Carpentras rite indicates that a number of liturgical poems were sung to vernacular tunes; see for instance the incipits to the piyyutim *Evkeh belev mar* and *Meqor-dem'ah eten 'einai* in *Seder le-arba' tzomot ule-arba' parshiyyot keminhaq q'q Carpentras* (Amsterdam, 1759-1762), fols. 109b-110b and 113b-114b.

³⁷ *The Lyrics of Thibaut of Champagne*, ed. and transl. Kathleen J. Brahney, Garland Library of Medieval Literature, vol. 41, Series A (New York and London: Garland, 1989), no. 54, pp. 232-33.

³⁸ Meir was writing at the height of Christian fervor (especially in northern France) for the cult of the Virgin. Indeed, one of the charges against the Talmud was that it contained insults to Mary. Donin's accusations in this regard provoked the only moment in the Talmud trial in which the proceedings were "tainted with rage and fear of violence"; see Jordan, "Marian Devotion," 63, 68, 75. See also David Berger, ed., *The Jewish-Christian Debate in the High Middle Ages: A Critical Edition of the Nizzahon Vetus* (Philadelphia: Jewish Publication Society, 1979), 302; Yerushalmi, "The Inquisition and the Jews," 357-63.

³⁹ *Selikhot, Minhag Ashkenaz* (Salonika, 1550), fol. 176. My thanks to Herbert Zafren and Noni Rudavsky of the Hebrew Union College Klau Library, who so generously aided me in locating this and other sources in the Klau collection.

⁴⁰ Leopold Zunz, *Literaturgeschichte der synagogalen Poesie* (Berlin: L. Gerschel Verlagsbuchhandlung, 1865), 591; Siegmund Salfeld, *Das Martyrologium des Nürnberger Memorbuches* (Berlin: L. Simion, 1898), 353. Salfeld tentatively identified the author with the Solomon b. Joseph who composed a lament for the martyrs of Anjou.

⁴¹ Isa 62:7; Micah 1:8.

⁴² Num 11:19; Micah 1:8.

⁴³ Ezek 7:17 or 21:12. The copyist erred, substituting *libbi bam* for *lemayim. Libbi.*

⁴⁴ Gen 31:29.

⁴⁵ Cf. Ezek 8:14, where Tammuz, however, is the name of a vegetation god who dies and revives each year.

⁴⁶ A. Habermann, *Gezerot ashkenaz vetsarefat*; H. Shirman, "Laments on the Persecutions in Eretz Yisrael, Africa, Spain, Ashkenaz and France" [in Hebrew], *Qobetz 'al yad* n.s. 3 (1939), 25-74; Bernfeld, *Sefer haDema'ot*; plus the laments

included in Salfeld, *Das Martyrologium*, and more recently in Daniel Goldschmidt and Avraham Fraenkel, *Leqet piyyutei-selihot*, 2 vols. (Jerusalem: Hotsaat Meqitsei nirdamim, 1993).

[47] Zunz dated Moses bar Nathan's lament, *Mimeitsar tsa'aqti*, to 1327; see Leser Landshuth, *Amude ha-Avodah* (Berlin, 1857-1862, reprint [Jerusalem?]: n.p., 1968), 256. However, among the manuscript sources Goldschmidt and Fraenkel cite for the poem are Parma, Biblioteca Palatina, MS. Parma 654, a Burgundy *mahzor* copied in 1304, and Oxford, Bodleian MS. Arch-Seld.A.3 (Neubauer 1159), a thirteenth-century codex.

[48] Bernfeld's excerpt from a 1096 lament, *Sefer haDema'ot*, 1:209, for the shoes; Meir of Rothenburg (attributed), *Ahbirah milin* for the drums, Habermann, *Gezerot ashkenaz vetsarefat*, 181-83. The latter example continues to bother me; Habermann reads the verses as a description of scrolls converted to drums, but I think, despite the difficulty of the verse, that it may describe the desecration of the scrolls while drums and music are played. The line reads:

תכס תורתך ומגלתך אכלה / לתופים ומחולות ולחורש- ברזל נתחללה / עד תום כל המגלה

Perhaps: "the wall of Your Torah, Your scroll, was consumed / to [the sound of?] drums and dances and iron rakes it was desecrated / until the scroll was finished."

[49] *Lamentations Rabbah*, 2.2, 3.39; the story is repeated in the *Babylonian Talmud*, Gittin 57b-58a.

[50] Mordecai bar Eleazer, *Ba'ti lefanekha*, in Habermann, *Gezerot ashkenaz vetsarefat*, 159-60; Bernfeld, *Sefer haDema'ot*, 1:258-62.

[51] Kalonymous bar Judah, *Mi yiten roshi mayim*, in Habermann, *Gezerot ashkenaz vetsarefat*, 66-69, and in Bernfeld, *Sefer haDema'ot*, 1:202-05.

[52] Ibid.

[53] The following summary relies on the discussions in Ephraim Urbach, "The Role of the French and Ashkenazic Sages in the Controversy over Maimonides and his Works" [in Hebrew], *Tarbiz* 12 (1947), 149-59; Joseph Shatzmiller, "Towards a Picture of the First Maimunist Controversy" [in Hebrew], *Tarbiz* 34 (1969),126-44; *idem*, "The Letter of R. Asher bar Gershom to the French Rabbis During the Maimunist Controversy" [in Hebrew], in *Mehqerim lezekher Tsvi Avineri*, ed. A. Gilboa et al. (Haifa: Univ. of Haifa, 1970), 129-40; and Azriel Shohet, "Clarifications Concerning the First Maimunist Controversy," 27-45.

[54] Indeed, Solomon b. Abraham reserved special wrath for Ibn Tibbon, *hama'atiq*, who by clarifying in his translation obscure passages in the original, increased the dangers posed by the text. Shohet, "Clarifications Concerning the First Maimunist Controversy," 29 (citing the letter of Solomon b. Abraham himself).

[55] Baer rejected his account of the burning. See Urbach, "The Role of the French and Ashkenazic Sages," 155.

[56] *Ta'am Zeqenim*, ed. Eleazer Ashkenazi (Frankfurt a.M.: I. Kauffman, 1854), 71. For the view that Hillel refers to massacres in Anjou (1236), see Margaliot's note

in the *Vikuah Rabbenu Yehiel*, 4, n. 23. See also Abraham David, "Riots against the French Jews during the Shepherds' Crusade of 1251" [in Hebrew], *Tarbiz* 46 (1977), 251-57. On 252, David discusses the reference in a liturgical poem, copied in 1242-1243, to great bloodshed in Paris, "the city of blood."

57 From Hillel's letter to the doctor Isaac, in *Ta'am Zeqenim*, ed. Ashkenazi, 70-73.

58 In addition to the letters of Ibn Hisdai and Hillel of Verona, a certain martyrological flavor may be detected in the Maimunists' assertions that R. Solomon b. Abraham and his cohorts were convicted as false witnesses and sentenced to lose their tongues. See the comment of Maimonides' son, Abraham, who collected and edited a group of the letters, in Shatzmiller, "Towards a Picture of the First Maimunist Controversy," 126, n. 5; the letter from Lunel, cited in Shatzmiller, "Towards a Picture of the First Maimunist Controversy," 135; the letter from the Ibn Hisdai brothers, in Solomon Joachim Halberstam, "The Religious War: A Collection of Letters concerning the Maimunist Controversy," *Jeschurun: Zeitschrift für die Wissenschaft des Judenthums* 8 (1871), 17-88, here 51; and the letter of Hillel of Verona, in *Ta'am Zeqenim*, ed. Ashkenazi, 71. Shohet assumes the claim is ridiculous, but Shatzmiller believes it is plausible. See Shohet, "Clarifications Concerning the First Maimunist Controversy," 45; Shatzmiller, "Towards a Picture of the First Maimunist Controversy," 135. The letter from the "sages" of Lunel and Narbonne to Spain describes the judicial procedure in convincing detail: "While the meat was still between their teeth, God grew angry with them, and their tongues brought about their downfall and disaster. They were arrested by the lord [?] and brought to the scaffold to be judged, and they were sentenced to have their tongues cut out. The king's servants rose against them in rage and took revenge. They stripped off their clothes, removed their shoes and tied their hands to their bodies. The prisoner's chain hung from their necks with a sharpened razor at their throats. The ban went before them saying, look, see the deeds of these sinners who testified falsely against members of their own faith. They brought them to the place of sentencing, and their tongues were cut off and they were banished in shame and disgrace from their city...." The letter is appended to Shatzmiller, "Towards a Picture of the First Maimunist Controversy," and this passage appears on page 141. It is tempting to wonder if the line in Solomon's poem "they stripped off their clothes and went barefoot" might refer to this incident.

59 The letter of the Ibn Hisdai brothers, sent to the Jewish communities in Castile and Aragon, in Halberstam, "The Religious War," 49.

60 From the Hebrew chronicle of Solomon bar Samson, in Habermann, *Gezerot ashkenaz vetsarefat*, 24.

61 Ibn Hisdai, in Halberstam, "The Religious War," 51; the punch line is cited by Hillel of Verona, in *Ta'am Zeqenim*, ed. Ashkenazi, 71. Since I have taken some liberty with the translation, I provide the Hebrew here:

קמו מורי שוא על מורה   צדק ונתנוהו חרץ

חלק לבם ויפרץ בם   האל פרץ לפני פרץ

31

[62] Such as the letter of Meir b. Todros HaLevi (censored by Abraham) and the response by R. Eleazer b. Judah of Worms (the "Rokeah"). See Urbach, "The Role of the French and Ashkenazic Sages," 150.

[63] Ibid, 42-44. At the same time, DaPiera also demonstrates that the fame of the Jewish martyrs from France and Ashkenaz had captured the attention (and admiration) of Jewish intellectuals in Spain. Why would these exemplars of faith martyr themselves, DaPiera asks, if (as his critics accused Maimonides of saying) there was no eternal reward or punishment? As for:

> Those who were slain for God's Name as a lesson in faith,
> My heart is with the mighty ones who were thus plundered.
> Why should these sages have submitted themselves to slaughter
> And redeemed their faith with their lives?

The passage is from no. 3, vv. 28-29; ed. Hayim Brody, "The Poems of Meshullam ben Solomon DaPiera" [in Hebrew], Yedi'ot haMakhon leHeqer haShirah ha'Ivrit 4 (1938): 17.

[64] Brody, "The Poems,"no. 15, p. 39, cited in Shohet, "Clarifications Concerning the First Maimunist Controversy," 43. For the poet's allusion, see Jer 23:28.

[65] Brody, "The Poems," from no. 44, p. 100. As Shohet, "Clarifications Concerning the First Maimunist Controversy," 44, n. 115, notes, Gershom Scholem dated these poems to the 1240s, without justifying the claim, but there is "no reason not to relate them to those years in which the controversy was at its height, that is, in the first half of the 1230s."

[66] The text is cited by Ephraim Urbach in his edition of Abraham b. Azriel's thirteenth-century compendium, the 'Arugat haBosem, 4 vols. (Jerusalem: "Meqitsei Nirdamim," 1963), 4:81. Haym Soloveitchik mentions the passage in "Three Themes in the Sefer Hasidim," AJS Review 1 (1976), 311-57, here 327.

[67] For the whole text, see I. Davidson, "Judah Ibn Shabbetai's Divrei ha-allah vehaniddui," HaEshkol 6 (n.d.), 165-75; the citation is taken from p. 167. See also Naftali Wieder, "The Burned Book of Judah Ibn Shabbetai" [in Hebrew], Metsudah 2 (1944), 123.

[68] See, for instance, the complaint of R. Samuel bar Solomon of Falaise, one of the official defenders of the Talmud in the trial of 1240, which is often cited as evidence of the success of the new policy. R. Samuel begins a response to a legal inquiry lamenting the shortage of books. He writes, "My spirit is wasted and my strength depleted; the Light of my eyes is gone because of the oppressor, whose hand has grown mighty against us. The soul and delight of our eyes was taken away, and we have no books from which we can gain enlightenment and understanding. May the Mighty One be zealous for His people and say we have suffered enough." The text is preserved in the collected responsa of Meir of Rothenburg (Prague ed.), no. 250; cited in Urbach, Ba'alei haTosafot, 377-78.

[69] Agus, Rabbi Meir of Rothenburg, 1:153, n. 122.

32

70 Yerushalmi, "The Inquisition and the Jews," 327. Yerushalmi connects this incident with the "lament" written by Kalonymous bar Kalonymous in his *Even Bohen*. Habermann believes the reference is to the Talmud burning of 1319; see Habermann's edition of the *Even Bohen* (Tel Aviv: Mahbarot le-sifrut,, 1956), 116 and the note on 161. The "lament" is not in verse. As did Meir's poem, this one relies on a trope first seen in Kalonymous bar Judah's 1096 lament. Here it is also adapted: "The Lord's perfect Law was sanctified on the day of her wedding and given to be burned" (p. 116).

71 Salo Baron, *A Social and Religious History of the Jews*, 18 vols. (New York: Columbia Univ. Press, 1965), 9:70, mentions the liturgy and *mahzor*, which is currently in the collection of the Jewish Theological Seminary in New York. My thanks to Menahem Schmelzer of the Seminary for forwarding me copies of the relevant folios. The source is JTS MS. 4510, fols. 304a-308a. The liturgy was apparently reused in Rome for a condemnation of the Talmud there.

72 The translation is based on the Hebrew text by Goldschmidt – see above, note 33. I have, however, numbered each half-line as a whole verse in order to maintain isomorphism with Shirman's numbering of the verses for HaLevi's poem.

73 Cf. 1Sam 30:3 (alluding to captured women). The "one burned in fire" is simultaneously the Torah (in its collective sense of oral and written law) and Zion, more specifically the burned Sanctuary in Zion's midst. By building his poem on HaLevi's lament, Meir links these figures inextricably. By the end of the poem, the female figure who is addressed seems to pick up echoes of the people (*bat-Zion*) as well.

74 In Amos 2:7, they who crush the poor (*sho'afim 'al 'afar eretz* in Amos and *sho'afim be'afar eretz* in Meir). The meaning of *sha'af* here implies to "gasp" or "pant" with desire; see Rashi's comment on the Amos verse, using the OF gloss *goloser*, "to desire ardently." See also the echo of this verse in HaLevi, *Tsion halo tishali*, v. 51, p. 488, *mibor shevi sho'afim negdekh* ("from captivity's pit they gasp for you").

75 Cf. HaLevi, *Tsion halo tishali*, vv. 49-50, p. 488: "… they feel pain / for your desolation" (*vehako'avim / 'al shomemutekh*), echoed in Meir's "feel pain" and "are stunned" (*vehako'avim hamishtomemim*).

76 Isa 50:10.

77 Isa 13:8.

78 Deut 9:3.

79 Cf. Isa 43:2.

80 O dainty foe (RSV: pleasure-lover) (*'adinah*), i.e., the enemy. See Isa 47:8. Chazan translates vv. 13-18 as directed to the Talmud/Torah, but this is improbable. The address sets a female personification of the enemy against the conflated female personification of "Torah" and Zion. See also Isa 30:15.

81 Prov 24:31 (the ground was covered with nettles). The "flowers" are an allusion to the *pirhei-kehunah* (lit., "flowers of the priesthood"), i.e., the students.

82 Ps 137:8.

[83] Flame and fire – Gen 15:17; Zech 12:6; but probably most intended is the Sinai imagery of Exod 20:15-23.

[84] Lit., so are you with your speech.

[85] Cf. HaLevi, *Tsion halo tishali,* vv. 29-30, p. 487 (" Mt. Hor, where there are two / great lights, your enlighteners and teachers").

[86] See the Targum to Isa 28:5 for *kelilah.*

[87] Prov 26:11 – as the dog returns to its vomit, the fool returns to (or "doubles") his folly.

[88] Exod 22:3, 6-8 and *Babylonian Talmud,* Baba Qama 7:1; Sanhedrin 1:1. According to Goldschmidt, 136, it is possible to read the verse as referring to "twofold damages" owed *to* Israel or *by* them. I think the pun also suggests that the "double" attack of the Christians corresponds to the double nature of Jewish Law (the Written and Oral traditions).

[89] Cf. Isa 33:4. See also HaLevi, *Tsion halo tishali,* vv. 39-40, p. 487 ("How can food or drink taste sweet when I see / that the dogs have dragged away your lions?").

[90] I have reordered the Hebrew phrases of vv. 38-40 to make sense in English. The allusion is to the mandated burning of booty taken from an idolatrous city *('ir nidahat);* see Deut 13:13-18. Chazan translates, "through your isolated quarter." The sense, however, is of a city or even a person who has been condemned and whose possessions are burned (as Chazan implies with his "holy booty," the goods are forbidden as personal spoil). "Those you have rejected from your congregation" – see Deut 23:3-4. The reference must be to the apostates who figured in the condemnation, chiefly Donin, who we recall was excommunicated by R. Yehiel in the 1230s.

[91] Lam 1:4.

[92] For the relation of this verse to HaLevi, *Tsion halo tishali,* v. 55, p. 488, see above, p. 8.

[93] Prov 7:19-20.

[94] See Rashi and the Targum to Cant 2:17, where "the shadows fled" is interpreted to mean that Israel sinned with the Golden Calf and therefore the shade of God's protection was removed.

[95] Isa 49:21.

[96] Literally, at the top of the mountain of your tower, drawing on Isa 30:17 ("like a mast on the top of a mountain").

[97] 2Sam 19:36.

[98] A mixed metaphor in Hebrew, reading literally "the cords of the drums of your pipes."

[99] Jer 15:8.

[100] Cf. HaLevi, *Tsion halo tishali,* v. 41, p. 487 ("How can the light of day be sweet to my eyes...").

[101] Destruction, as in Jer 17:18; lit., brokenness, as in Ezek 21:11.

[102] Jer 2:2.

34

[103] I.e., to divide the people and destroy its leaders.

[104] Ps 90:15, and for the particular use of 'enut, Ps 22:25.

[105] For *shefel* as a condition of lowliness, see Ps 136:23 ("in our degradation, He remembered us").

[106] Cf. Isa 49:18; Exod 15:20.

[107] Ps 18:29; Isa 58:10.